MY
DEFIANT CHILD

A Peace Over Conflict Parenting Approach to Nurture Your Disobedient Child.

Jane Hawkins

TABLE OF CONTENTS

Introduction

Parenting in and of itself is an overwhelmingly challenging experience. Add to it the difficult experience of raising a child with behavioral concerns, and you find yourself in a uniquely perplexing situation. Isolation, guilt, fear, disappointment, worry, anger, and many other emotions are all entirely natural when you are parenting a child with a behavioral disorder. While all parents will experience challenges in their parenting journey, none are quite the same as the challenges presented by a child with a tendency to be defiant.

Discussions around behavioral disorders have become far less taboo in recent years, enabling parents gateways to a broader spectrum of support than they once did. Still, many of these subjects are difficult to comment on, as not everyone is open for discussion. Accessing the guidance you require alongside receiving adequate support may feel practically impossible as you confront struggles that are quite unique from other parents. Sadly, it can force you to relentlessly question yourself as a parent, as the methods that work for other families do not work for you and your child. Without appropriate support, these battles you're contending with can make parenting a tremendously challenging experience; emotionally, physically, and mentally.

In *'My Defiant Child'* I seek to provide you with guidance for resolving defiant and behavioral concerns while designing a more tranquil environment for yourself and your family. Learning how to form a more peaceful atmosphere will grant you and your family access to a more positive, enjoyable space to co-exist. Through these shifts, it will become far easier for you to guide, teach, and raise your child in a positive manner, while experiencing the true joys of parenting.

Whether you have been experiencing troubles right from the start, or they are related to a recent growth spurt, there is no reason why you should not be able to experience relief from these challenges. Through adjustments in your mindset, a deeper understanding of how you can support your child, and more effective parenting strategies, you can discover the best way to parent your child with success.

If you are ready to bridge the gap between yourself and your child and enjoy more freedom and greater results as a parent, let's begin!

Chapter One:

You Love Your Child

I want to start by acknowledging the most important element that people commonly overlook: you love your child. Yes, your child may be challenging, and catering to their needs may seem like a laundry list of tasks that parents with neurotypical children could not possibly comprehend. Yet, regardless of these additional challenges, you love your child.

You, like every other parent on earth, spent time anticipating the birth of your beautiful child. Whether you gave birth to them biologically, gave birth through surrogacy, or adopted your child, you looked forward to the presence of that precious baby as much as any other parent did. You dreamt of what they would be like, how they would grow up, the type of relationship you would share, and the many ways you would cherish each other's presence. Just because your child has a behavioral disorder does not mean they were, or are, any less wanted, cherished, or loved.

Upon discovering that your child had a behavioral disorder, you may have felt a whirlwind of different emotions. Each one rooted in the very same emotion: love. You love your child so much that you worried about their safety, feared what life would be like for them, became angry with the fate they were dealt, and grieved the life they may never have. Every emotion you have felt as a result of this diagnosis, regardless of what emotion that was or how it felt, was born out of pure love for your child.

It is love that has you sitting here right now, discovering how you can parent your child in a way that suits their unique needs. Despite how distressed, overwhelmed, frustrated, or miserable, you may be with parts of your parenting, all you care about is making the experience more peaceful for everyone involved. You recognize that if you can increase your own peace, you will increase your child's peace, too. And, if you can increase your child's peace, you can improve the quality of their life, your life, the life of your entire family, and the relationship you share with your precious child. You are here, not because you are fed up and have no idea as to where to turn, but because you are ready to implement new ideas in a more positive, impactful way. You are ready to experience that freedom, and more importantly, you are ready to watch your child experience the freedom of a life without misery and meltdowns.

You love your child so much that in light of all of the hardships you have faced, you hold onto the most significant emotion you could have: hope. You hope for a brighter future, a better quality of life, and a more effortless ability for your child to learn how to fit into the world around them in a way that fits their unique needs. That hope you carry is strong enough to start creating the exact results you want, and need, and is precisely what will assist you in being the exact parent your child needs.

I know it can be tremendously difficult. You may move through many emotions, possibly even on a day to day basis. At times, you feel full of that precious hope and confidence that you have everything under control, and you can make things work. Sometimes, you feel worried about your child and fear what their future will look like, and that fear may make you feel angry, withdrawn, overprotective, or even hopeless for a short period of time. Occasionally, you may even feel angry, frustrated, or downright furious with the situation. You may take it out on your child through the form of resentment, disappointment, stress, and heartache, which inevitably leads to you feeling guilty, embarrassed, and even ashamed. You have no desire to feel these feelings toward your child, but you resent what has happened to them, and it manifests as resentment toward the entire experience. This encourages you to try harder, push yourself further, and become the parent they need you to be. Hopefully, you can use this motivation to stop feeling those feelings of resentment and hold onto that feeling of having everything figured out a little more often. You know that, regardless of what happens, you love your child more than anything, and those feelings are only feelings.

Before we can proceed into practical strategies that will transform your parenting experience, we need to discuss your feelings. Feelings around parenting children with a behavioral disorder can be distressing, as they are directly related to one of the most precious things in your entire life. Unlike parents who have neurotypical children who may experience occasional guilt when they overreact to a challenge, parents of children with behavioral disorders tend to feel massive amounts of guilt and distress. Your guilt may be coming from many areas, ranging from your seeming failure to create a more harmonious environment, to your inability to take away your child's sorrow and make life easier for them, or even the way you feel about parenting in general. You must always remember that all of these feelings are normal, and they are *just feelings*. Feeling resentful toward your child for a challenging day does not mean that you resent your child, or that you have any reason to feel guilty. It does mean that you had a stressful day, and your brain reacted naturally by creating a resistance toward the trigger of that stress, which unfortunately happens to be your child. Remind yourself anytime you feel these feelings, especially when they begin to feel troubling, that you have *not* fallen into a place of hating your child. *You love your child.* Your emotions prove you love your child because you care so much about their wellbeing that you have an emotional reaction anytime you realize they are not doing as well as they could be. As you discover healthier coping methods, you will find ways to improve your child's quality of life and, therefore, your own. Those feelings of resentment, stress, disappointment, worry, fear, frustration, guilt, and other troubling feelings will not entirely disappear, but they will be significantly minimized as a result.

To begin coping with your emotions in a healthier manner, start by taking a few deep breaths and reminding yourself of just how much you love your child. You anticipated your baby, dreamed about counting their little fingers and toes, and stared into their eyes the first time with the greatest hope, excitement, fear, and *love* you had ever experienced in your life. Your child, your baby, is special to you, and no amount of temporary feelings can take away from the fact that you love your child. Remember that.

Anytime you find yourself feeling wound up, overwhelmed, drained, or guilty for having any of these feelings in the first place, think back to the first time you laid eyes on them, their first smile, or their first laugh. Cherish the wonderful memories that remind you of how precious they are, and use that to ground yourself in the reality that your feelings are temporary. Still, your love will withstand everything, no matter how challenging it may be.

Practicing the new techniques I will teach you, will help in navigating those situations less dramatically so you can avoid screaming bouts and meltdowns. As you start to feel a more profound sense of peace in your parenting methods, and you see your child positively responding to your changes, you will begin to experience far fewer overwhelming emotions. You *can* do it, and things *will* get better. It just takes time.

Chapter Two:

Change Starts With You (The Parent)

Parenting your child correctly, regardless of whether your child is neurotypical or lives with a behavioral disorder, means you have to create a parenting style that matches the needs of your child. Many first-time parents believe that they can choose their parenting style in advance and that their technique will automatically suit their child simply because that is the parenting style that feels best for them.

Your child will come out with their own personality, preferences, strengths, weaknesses, and needs. You, as the parent, must create an adaptable parenting style that meets those needs so you can empower your child to grow up to be the best version of themselves they can be. For parents of neurotypical children, the example of how they want their children to become seems pretty clear-cut. For parents of children with behavioral disorders, your expectations may be different based on the level of ability that your child has. There is no right or wrong here, so long as you have created expectations that are reasonable for your child to live up to. The goal is not to turn your child into who you want them to be, but to help them flourish into the best version of themselves they can become. When you realize that, it becomes easier to accept any version of your child that this may be, even if it does not match the "typical" outlook for a child. There is no such thing as a typical outlook, anyway.

Creating Healthy Expectations

If you approach parenting with a pre-existing ideology for how your child should be as an adult, you will fail your child. Of course, it's hard not to have expectations of your child, especially when you envisioned a future that you hope will keep them happy and fulfilled. Every parent, no matter who they are, has expectations for their child. The problem is, your expectations are not your child's responsibility to live up to. Further, when your child truly cannot live up to those expectations, holding onto them only worsens the amount of stress and disappointment you feel as their parent. Not toward them, but toward the fear that they will not experience happiness and fulfillment because you were confident that your way was *the* way for them to experience it.

First of all, I want you to release the idea that there is only one way to be happy and fulfilled. Secondly, let go of your current expectations and become more flexible in the image you have for your child. Instead of the life you had initially pictured, visualize a realistic future for them that would enable your child to reach their fullest potential, one that you as a family collective can help to shape and influence to bring out their best. If your child can, involve them in this stimulating process so they can have a hands-on role in creating the dream for their future, too. Make it fun, make it interesting, gather as much input from them as possible. If your child is not able, consider involving their doctors or therapists in your vision to get a more robust understanding of what a realistic and reasonable image looks like in the first place.

When you have genuine expectations for your child, you can break down the ultimate dream into smaller achievable goals for you and your child to work toward. This is the big difference between realistic and unrealistic expectations. If you were parenting with unrealistic expectations for example, you could open up a life of ongoing frustration, stress, and sadness as your child cannot reasonably meet those expectations. When you parent with realistic expectations, however, you see lovely progress toward those goals, and you begin to feel a sense of pride, accomplishment, and fulfillment with your child. That positive energy will be felt by your child, too, and it will lead to greater harmony between the two of you, as well as a deeper bond that you can both share. This energy will further increase the level of success you experience with parenting your child and aiding them in becoming the best they can be.

Understanding the Role of Emotions

Emotions are a biological reaction that everyone, including parents, experience. Your feelings are part of your primal brain, and they help you survive by creating protective reactions within your body. For example, let's say you experience a situation that cultivates the sensation of fear within you. That fear will affect your thoughts by creating a sense of panic, which will subsequently heighten your senses and alert you to any surrounding dangers. This system is designed to protect you. Your body will experience changes and adapt in an effort to endure the incoming threat. An emotion like fear will increase your heart rate, dilate your pupils, and bring on the production of hormones like adrenaline and cortisol, which temporarily spike your energy levels so you can fight or flight, depending on the circumstances.

As modern humans, we have advanced beyond imagination, and tend to rely less on this survival system as opposed to our ancestors or the likes of wild animals facing life-threatening situations daily. Regardless, it is still ingrained deep within our DNA, and it still has a significant impact on us. You, as the parent, can begin to feel symptoms of chronic stress, worry, anxiety, depression, fear, anger, and other emotions relating to parenting anytime you are in a parenting situation. For example, when your child has a meltdown, you may become aggravated and overwhelmed before the meltdown has even fully begun because you are anticipating what is coming. This routine reaction to the trigger of your child having a meltdown is intended to protect you from a negative emotional situation, which is why your emotions become overwhelming. Understand that this is completely natural.

Your child experiences sensations similarly. They, too, have their triggers that lead them to believe they are about to face negative emotions. Children already have difficulty regulating their feelings, but those with behavioral disorders may have even more significant challenges. When your child is triggered, they may turn from 0 to 100 in a matter of moments because, on a biological level, they believe their wellbeing is threatened. Intentionally acting defiant is not their objective, they are responding to a natural physiological reaction occurring within their body.

As their parent, you need to be aware of how your emotions are affecting your child's experience and how their perceived negative experience contributes to their meltdowns. When you realize that their reactions are biological and not intentionally malicious, it becomes easier to have compassion in that moment and release your own negative emotions, first. In doing so, you create a safe and peaceful atmosphere for your child, allowing them to calm down, too.

Putting Your Safety Mask on First

As the parent of a child with a behavioral disorder, you have likely been presented with many situations where you had to defend your child in unusual ways. You have had to protect your child mentally, emotionally, and physically from many involvements they have encountered that are not ordinary experiences for neurotypical children. Perhaps you have protected them by drastically adjusting their environment, dealing with bullies at day-care/school, or fending off fellow adults that do not comprehend your child or your parenting experience at all. All of these occurrences can be exhausting and seemingly never-ending when you are protecting your child. They can also leave you forgetting to tend to yourself and your own emotions as you become absorbed with protecting your child from the world around them.

You have to remember to put your "safety mask" on first.

While defending your child occurs naturally, it is vital that you remember that you cannot help your child to your truest potential if you, yourself are not thriving. Whether it's protecting them from bullies or helping them navigate the world around them, if you have worn yourself thin by constantly shielding them from everything, without ever stopping to take care of yourself, you will become burnt out. That burn out will lead to far more challenging emotions for you to navigate within yourself, which will inevitably lead to far greater complications during the more challenging moments of parenting, too.

Putting your safety mask on first does not mean lessening your time spent caring for your child. It means caring for them in a way that enables you to take care of yourself, too, which deepens your ability to be there for them and protect them. To care for yourself first, start by considering your mental and emotional health. Recognize how challenging the emotions of parenting a child with a disorder can be, and give yourself the space and support you need to navigate those emotions by taking breaks, practicing active stress-management, and talking to someone if you need to. The more you can regulate your own emotions, the easier it will be to regulate yourself and your child during would-be meltdowns and complex circumstances.

Accepting Mistakes As an Opportunity to Learn

You, like every other parent, are bound to make mistakes. You have probably already made thousands by now, and there will be plenty more as you continue your journey of parenting. Even parents of adult children make mistakes and find themselves having to recover from those mistakes in one way or another, as mistakes are a natural part of raising children. As they say, children do not come with a manual.

Rather than punishing yourself for making mistakes, or having an unrealistic outlook of your ability to parent without making mistakes, you need to accept the fact that mistakes are inevitable. You will make mistakes many times over, whether you like it or not. Sometimes, you will become overwhelmed and will have difficulty regulating your emotions. Other times, you might miss an important cue, and it could lead to your child having a meltdown and your environment lacking the peace you strive to create. There are many ways that mistakes can be made, and many reasons why those mistakes may be made. Regardless of how they happen, though, you must understand that they are inevitable.

Learn to adapt to each situation, developing new strategies for how you will minimize the impact of your errors on future experiences. Shift your perspective to view mistakes as an opportunity to learn and grow as a parent. Every time you overreact, miss a cue, or have a negative experience with parenting, reflect on why that happened, and what contributed to your negative experience. See if you can identify the trigger, the moment where everything went wrong, and what could have been done to prevent that situation or reverse it once it started. When you use mistakes as motivation for learning, it becomes easier to forgive yourself and navigate any new challenges thrown at you in a more prepared, productive, and calm state if similar situations were to arise.

Increasing Your Feelings of Gratitude

Upon confronting chronically challenging situations, it can be easy to develop negative mindsets toward those circumstances. With parenting your child, you may have negative emotions toward parenting, the day to day experiences you have with your child, or even your child themselves. Again, these are only feelings caused by troubling emotions, and they do not reflect the way you truly feel about your child. Still, if they linger long enough, it can make the entire experience of parenting far more frustrating and can damage your relationship with your child, as well as the way you behave toward and around your child.

Taking time to regularly express appreciation for your child's existence and for the opportunity as a parent is an important way to counter those negative feelings so that you can create a more realistic and positive parenting experience. Each day, express gratitude to yourself and your child.

You could express gratitude for:

- Getting through the day
- Having the will to discover healthier skills
- The existence of your child
- The support you have from your partner/family/friends/your therapist/anyone else who supports you
- Access to resources to improve your experience
- The love you have for your child
- A positive moment you shared with your child

Or anything else that helps you feel gratitude around parenting, your ability to parent, your relationship with your child, or your child themselves.

To your child, you should express gratitude for their existence and for them being in your life. Regularly letting your child know that you love them, are grateful for them, and appreciate them expands their self-esteem and self-confidence, and these boosts significantly improve their overall wellbeing. Studies have also shown that children who have a higher sense of self-worth and confidence have a more exceptional ability to learn, grow, and mature in a positive way.

Chapter Three:

Your Child's Precious Developing Brain

E very child goes through several growth spurts throughout their lifetime. Growth spurts often happen every few days in newborns, every few weeks in babies, every few months in toddlers and younger children, and every few years in older children. When your child has a behavioral disorder, it can affect the way they reach their developmental milestones and their willingness to adapt to any milestones they are coming upon. Your child may be especially cranky or put off during these times because they are experiencing changes they cannot describe, as well as difficulty with regulating their emotions surrounding those changes.

Understanding what developmental milestones are, and how your child may reach them or experience them differently, helps you understand why they are experiencing such difficulty and how that difficulty is leading to behavioral complications. It is important to recognize that the behavioral outbursts are not chosen, nor is it the result of a child not *wanting* to behave. Realizing that this is not a willed behavior, but a biological behavior can help you refrain from blaming your child or forcing them to see things your way because you have more compassion for the fact that they simply cannot.

Often, behavioral disorders are discovered because milestones are not being adequately met, or they are being met with great difficulty. If this is how you found your child's behavioral disorder, you may already have awareness around the fact that these developments are more challenging for your child. Educating yourself on what is going on within their brain can support you with assisting them through various milestones and helping them with their growth and development.

Babyhood Milestones

The significant milestones in babyhood are at one month, three months, seven months, and one year. While it will seem like your child achieves a new milestone every week, this is how doctors break it down into easy to organize, bite-sized pieces. If your child doesn't hit these milestones it's okay, sometimes they can also just be slightly delayed.

By one month, your baby has achieved milestones like moving their body around, although it will be with jerky motions. They should also be able to bring their hands in front of their eyes and mouth, keep their hands in tight fists, and have sharp reflexes. Their eyes will likely wander and cross; they prefer black and white or high contrast patterns and will prefer human faces over anything else. By now, their hearing is fully mature, and they may recognize some sounds or turn their face toward familiar voices. They may also clearly avoid bitter or acidic scents and favor sweet smells. If there is a problem at one month, your baby may have trouble feeding, they may not blink when shown a bright light, or they may lack focus and seem unable to follow a nearby object side to side with their eyes. They may also appear stiff, without moving their arms or legs much, or come across as too floppy or even limp when being held. If their lower jaw always trembles or they do not startle or respond to loud noises, this is not a good indication, either.

By three months, your baby should be able to raise their head and chest when lying on their stomach and support their upper body with their arms. They should also be able to stretch their legs out and kick when lying either on their stomach or back, while their hands should regularly open and shut. A three-month-old should also be able to swipe at toys hanging above them and grasp at and shake hand toys. They will also be intently observing faces, recognizing familiar faces and objects, babbling, imitating certain sounds, and turning their head toward sounds. Three month old's can smile, pick favorite people, and will try harder to communicate and express themselves through their bodies. If your child is not responding to sounds, not noticing her hands, not smiling at people, not babbling, and not bringing objects to his mouth by four months, this may indicate something is wrong. A baby who does not try to imitate any noises, who does not push down with their feet when they are on a firm surface, or who has trouble moving their eyes in a specific direction or keeps their eyes crossed most of the time is also showing red flags.

By seven months, your baby should be able to roll onto their back and front, sit without support, support their weight on their whole legs, and transfer objects from one hand to another. They should see in color, see at a distance, and track moving objects with ease. A seven-month-old can also reply to their name, respond to the word "no," and distinguish emotion by the tone of voice. They also respond to sound with their own sounds, use their voice to express themselves, and consistently babbles. By seven months old, your baby should be able to find partially hidden objects, explore the world around them using their hands and mouth, and struggle to reach for objects beyond reach. They should also enjoy social play, mirror images, and other people's expressions. If your baby seems stiff or limp, is unable to hold themselves in a sitting position, is unwilling to cuddle, only uses one hand, shows no affection for their caregivers, or avoids/dislikes being around other people, these are red flags. Babies who have difficulty responding to sounds, moving objects toward their mouth, turning their head to locate sounds, roll over, laugh or squeal, follow objects with their eyes, or bear weight on their legs by seven months are also showing red flags.

By one year, your baby should be able to get into sitting position without assistance, crawl, assume the hand-and-knees position, creep on their hand and knees, move between positions easily, pull themselves into a standing position, and walk along furniture. They may also be able to stand for a few moments without support or even take a few steps. One year old's should be banging toys together, poking with their index finger, voluntarily releasing objects, putting objects into containers, and scribbling on paper on their own. They should be able to say "mama" and "dada" as well as exclamations like "oh-oh!" and they will likely try to imitate words, as well. A one-year-old is curious, has developed a stronger sense of cognitive permanence, and may express shyness or anxiety around strangers. They will also likely cry when their parents leave, imitate others, have unique preferences and dislikes, the ability to test parental responses, and the ability to finger-feed themselves. They may also extend an arm or a leg to help you put their clothes on. If a one year old cannot crawl, drags one side of the body when crawling for longer than a month, or cannot stand with support, this is a red flag. You should also be concerned if your child cannot say single words, search for hidden objects, use gestures for communication, or point to objects and pictures.

Two-Year-Old Milestones

By two years old, your child should be able to walk alone, pull toys behind them, carry larger toys, or run. They will also start standing on their tiptoes, kicking balls, climbing onto and off of furniture without assistance, using the stairs, scribbling, turning over containers to empty contents, building towers with multiple blocks, and using their preferred hand. When a picture is named for them, a two-year-old should be able to point out that picture. They should also recognize familiar names, objects, and body parts, say several single words, use simple phrases, and use two to four word sentences. Two year old's can follow simple instructions, repeat overheard words in conversation, find well-hidden objects, sort shapes and colors, and play make-believe. Socially and emotionally, two year old's imitate other's behaviors, are aware of their individuality, get enthusiastic about the company of other children, demonstrate increasing independence, express defiance, and experience more separation anxiety.

If something is wrong developmentally, you will notice it through your child's behavior. If a two-year-old struggles to walk, fails to develop a proper heel-toe walking pattern, cannot speak at least fifteen words, or cannot use two-word sentences by two, there is a red flag. An inability to name common household objects, imitate actions or words, follow simple instructions, or push a wheeled toy by age two is also reason for concern.

Four-Year-Old Milestones

Four year old's have accomplished many milestones at this point in their lives. A four-year-old should be able to stand on one foot for up to five seconds, go up and down stairs without support, kick a ball, throw a ball overhand, and move forward and backward with agility. They can copy square shapes, draw people with two to four body parts, use scissors, draw circles, and copy some capital letters. A four year old's language milestones include the ability to understand the concept of "same" and "different," an understanding of the basic rules of grammar, the ability to speak in five to six-word sentences, clear language, and the ability to tell stories. They can also correctly name colors, understand the concept of counting, approach problems from a single point of view, experience a clearer sense of time, follow three-part commands, recall parts of stories, and engage in fantasy play. Four-year-old social and emotional milestones include an interest in new experiences, the ability to cooperate with other children, a desire to play "mom" or "dad" in fantasy play, inventive fantasy play, the ability to dress and undress, and the capacity to negotiate solutions to conflicts. Four year old's are also more independent, can imagine monsters, will view themselves as a whole individual with a body, mind, and feelings, and cannot always distinguish between fantasy and reality.

If your four-year-old cannot throw a ball overhand, jump in place or ride a tricycle, grasp a crayon properly, scribble, stack multiple blocks, or copy a circle, this is a red flag. Four year old's that are still clingy when their parents leave, show no interest in interactive games, ignore other children, ignore other's outside of the family, fail to engage in fantasy play, resist dressing, sleeping, or using the toilet, or that lash out without self-control when they are angry are also showing red flags. Two additional red flags to look out for include the inability to use sentences with more than three words, or the inability to use "you" and "me" appropriately.

Five-Year-Old Milestones

Five years old marks another point for many major milestones to be met in a child's life. By five, children can usually stand on one foot for ten seconds or longer, hop and do somersaults, use swings, climb, and may even be able to skip. They can copy triangles, draw people with bodies, print some letters, dress and undress without assistance, use forks, spoons, and occasionally a butter knife. They can also take care of their own toilet needs. In regards to language, five year old's can recall parts of stories, speak sentences of more than five words, use future tense, tell longer stories, and recite their name and address. Cognitively, five year old's can count ten or more objects, name at least four colors, understand the concept of time better, and maintains knowledge about several everyday household items. In concern to social and emotional skills, a five-year-old wants to please and mimic their friends. They are also more likely to agree to rules, sing, dance, and act, show independence such as by visiting a friend on their own, become aware of their sexuality, can distinguish fantasy from reality, and can fluctuate between being demanding and being eagerly cooperative.

If your five-year-old is extremely fearful, timid, or aggressive, or still has an incredibly hard time separating from his or her parents, this is a red flag. Five year old's who are easily distracted, lack concentration, show little interest in other children, refuse to respond to others, rarely use fantasy or imitation play, seem unhappy or sad most of the time are showing red flags. Other red flags at five years old include aloof behavior around other children and adults, a limited range of emotions, difficulty eating, sleeping, or using the toilet, inability to differentiate between reality and fantasy, unusually passive behavior, or an inability to understand two-part commands. Some parents also note that their children cannot correctly provide their first and last name, use plurals or past tense, talk about their daily activities, build towers with multiple blocks, comfortably hold a crayon, take off their clothes, brush their teeth, or wash and dry their hands. All of these are indications that something may be wrong and are areas where a child with a behavioral disorder may struggle to keep up with their peers.

Milestones Beyond This Point

By five years old, most children who have behavioral disorders have now been checked out and had their disorders identified or symptoms remedied. At this point, you may have noticed that your child is clearly not reaching the same milestones as their peers, or is reaching them with difficulty. If any concerns remain it is advised to seek the assistance of your doctor.

A child diagnosed with a behavioral disorder can be distressing at first because, as a parent, you wish to see your child excel. Realizing they are falling behind from their peers can bear overwhelming emotions and remain difficult to witness. You might also find your child struggling to accept that they are different, or possibly even completely unaware of the fact they are unlike those around them, both of which are challenging in their own ways.

The best way to help your child is to discuss your milestones with their doctor and request that the doctor support you in identifying upcoming milestones whilst also determining the most efficient pathway to success. For children who resist milestones or who seem completely disinterested, there may be ways that you can increase your child's interest and encourage them to learn new ideas alongside their peers. For children who seem to struggle with regulating themselves and become overwhelmed or triggered by new concepts, there may be methods you can implement to help them relieve their stress and experience more peace from their emotions.

Knowing your child's unique behavioral disorder and how it tends to affect children in general, alongside keeping track of how it has already affected your child, will help you gain a more acute and precise solution. Knowing this, you gain confidence that you can support your child in the way they need at all stages of their developmental journey. This also supports you with having realistic and reasonable expectations that create a more impactful parenting experience for you, too.

Chapter Four:

No Drama Discipline Methods

C hildren with behavioral disorders are recognized to struggle with disciplinary action. Neurotypical children will often experience discipline as a means to prevent them from committing unwanted action, and while they will react to it, their reactions are often predictably common considering their situation. Children who have behavioral disorders, however, struggle to maintain standardized emotional responses to correction. Unfortunately, these children may also find themselves suffering disciplinary action far more frequently since they struggle to engage in typical behavior or healthily regulate themselves. A child who tends to resist milestones, for example, might be disciplined for not taking action, while a child who struggles to regulate their emotions may be punished for excessive emotional reactions such as outbursts of aggression.

As a parent, you may seek to ascertain an appropriate balance for discipline. On one hand, you know you need to use control to correct your child's behavior, but on the other, you understand that your child does not reason or behave like a typical child, and this can create a perplexing situation. How do you know when to discipline your child? How do you educate your child? And when you do, and they start melting down, how do you navigate those defiant outbreaks?

Children with behavioral disorders rarely respond to discipline well, which leads to the parents dealing with enormous amounts of drama in their homes. You may feel like you are walking on eggshells because you are afraid of triggering your child and setting off a meltdown, or experiencing the harsh consequences of your child's anger.

Unearthing a means that you can safely and effectively discipline your child is a life-changing experience for parents of children who tend to be more defiant than others. The knowledge to provide your child positive guidance, and deter them from unwanted behaviors, without having a full-blown meltdown is an exceptional skill to grasp. This allows you to show your child how they can partake in day to day activities with a more positive approach, experience more affirmative attention from the people around them, and enjoy a higher quality of life in general. Effectively disciplining your child means you gain the ability to truly parent your child in a way that directly matches their needs and increases your ability to get them to the point of becoming the best possible version of themselves.

Maximize Positive Attention for Your Child

A neurodivergent child often receives a great deal of negative attention from the world around them. For many of these children, something as simple as having a negative reaction to their surroundings can leave them questioning themselves and the world around them. Having a life constantly filled with overwhelming events, punishment, and a negative stigma from society can be extremely exhausting. Further, it feels like no one is rooting for them, so your child does not feel overly compelled to listen to anyone or please anyone.

If your child has a behavioral disorder, you need to increase the amount of positive attention they receive. Consistent positive affirmation on a day to day basis can improve your child's relationship with yourself, as well as other adults, and in turn improves the likelihood of your child listening to what you have to say. Running around outside, playing games with family members, or cooperating on a fun project together are all great ways to generate positive attention with your child. Regardless of how your child has behaved, ensure that you always create this time for them. This expresses that you love them unconditionally and desire to share encouraging, meaningful interactions together irrespective of how they have behaved. When they recognize that you adore them at all costs and cherish every moment together, they grow more willing and eager to please you. Therefore, they will try considerably harder to listen and abide to the tasks you ask of them without fuss.

When you gift your child positive attention, ensure that they receive at least 15 minutes of your undivided attention every day. This gentle consideration reduces their tendency to try to capture your attention using negative behavior, rendering to fewer spurs to discipline your child in the first place. The most efficient method to stop a tantrum is to prevent one in the first place, not by giving in to your child and letting them get away with anything to avoid the outburst, but by providing your child with an environment that they thrive in.

Avoid Power Struggles

Children with behavioral disorders may engage in lengthy and exhausting power struggles with their parents, to get their way. Power struggles are signs of a child wanting to be in control of their own life and expecting everything to go their way regardless of what is right or wrong. In some cases, such as with children who have ODD or ADHD, they may be particularly wise at luring you into lengthy debates that end in a power struggle. As the parent, you must avoid these power struggles because regardless of how they seem, they are not productive or helpful to your situation in any shape or form.

Anytime you ask your child to complete a task, and they combat your direction, refrain from engaging back and forth in a debate. The longer you are arguing with your child, the longer it takes them to clean their room, brush their teeth or get ready for an outing. Instead of arguing, provide your child with clear instructions and clear consequences they will have to face if they do not clean their room, and if your commands are not fulfilled, follow through on those consequences.

Never attempt to force your child to complete a task. Nagging, arguing, or yelling at your child will remain entirely ineffective. Instead, set clear boundaries that make it unpleasant for them to ignore your requests and let them know after one warning that if they do not listen, they will face those unpleasant consequences. Always follow through, your child must respect your word and your authority. Otherwise, your bluff will be called, and the acts of defiance will develop considerably worse as your child learns to outmaneuver your leniency.

Create Clear, Easy to Follow Rules

Children with autism may struggle with rules because they do not comprehend, seemingly forget or lack awareness of them entirely. Children with behavioral disorders like ODD or ADHD know what the rules are but will often willingly defy them or argue about them, looking for a way to push your buttons and break the rules altogether to suit their agenda.

A great way to reduce disagreements and minimize meltdowns is to establish clear household rules and regularly remind your child of them. Again, refrain from engaging in power struggles around these rules by refusing to argue about them, instead of having clear-cut consequences of what will happen if your child fails to respect those rules. It can be highly effective to post the household rules in a prominent area of your house, such as on your fridge, so your child can see them each day. If required, refer to the list of rules to remind your child of what the household guidelines are, as this prevents them from arguing with you and helps them behave by giving them something clear and focused to reflect on.

When it comes to household rules, avoid making them too complicated or extensive. Use a few basic rules and keep them clear and straightforward. Excellent rules include: "Do your homework, finish your chores, go to bed on time and without a fuss, and respect yourself and everyone around you." These are basic, easy to follow, and create a clear sense of instruction for your child, which will also help minimize the instance of drama by reducing the number of things your child has to argue or meltdown about in the first place.

Have a Plan for Addressing Their Behavior

Your child's behavioral concerns will be solely unique to them. While parents of children with the same disorder will be able to relate with you, no two children are the same, and therefore, no parent will be able to understand what you are going through completely. You should not rely on a one-size-fits-all approach to dealing with your child.

Instead of trying to fit them into a cookie-cutter approach, focus on creating a behavioral plan that specifically meets the needs of your child. An excellent way to create a robust and well-rounded plan that is reasonable for your child to follow is by creating one with their doctor and therapists. This way, your child's doctor and therapists can also discuss the strategy and information relating to it, hopefully helping your child get on the right track and follow your requests more easily.

Behavioral plans should address arguments, aggression, talking back, refusing to do homework, temper tantrums, resistance toward necessary tasks, emotional concerns, and any other behavioral concerns your child has. They should be as comprehensive as possible and should cover all of the significant areas of concern that you have, as this ensures that you are equipped to navigate any situation that may arise.

When a behavioral plan has been prepared, it should include consequences that they will receive when they break the rules, and these consequences should be clearly explained ahead of time so that your child is well aware of what to expect. Often, these clear expectations avoid many meltdowns because your child already knows what to expect; therefore, they are less likely to try and push your boundaries. However, they may still try the first few times until they discover that you are not budging on your decision to enforce the promised consequences. Once they know you mean what you say, they will become far more likely to listen.

In addition to creating a behavioral plan for bad behavior, you should also discuss a behavioral plan for good behavior. Reward systems, positive attention, expressions of gratitude and appreciation, and other similar approaches should encourage your child to continue engaging in ethical behavior. When your child discovers that lousy behavior or unwanted behavior is unpleasant and painful to maintain, and ethical behavior or wanted action is pleasant and celebrated, they will naturally want to shift toward good behavior. This works directly with their basic biology, rather than just the logical part of their brain, which means that no matter how complex your child's behavioral disorder might be, this certainly will be effective in supporting you.

Be Consistent with Your Consequences

Delivering consequences to your child may seem difficult to follow through with. However, it is essential that if you promise a specific set of consequences to a child, you follow through on those consequences if they are disobeyed. Children with behavioral disorders will be far more likely to try to trigger your emotions and encourage you to cave to their preferences, and the minute they spot your weaknesses, they will seek to manipulate any vulnerabilities to get their way. This is not necessarily intentionally malicious, but is ingrained as a part of their way of thinking.

Showing your child that there are indeed consequences and that those consequences will be followed through on every single occasion ensures that your child envisions you your word as fact. Understand that children with behavioral disorders do not think like neurotypical children. In relation to consequences, for example, a child with a behavioral disorder that believes there is a one in one hundredth chance that a meltdown could help them get their way, *will* commit to that meltdown. If you succumb to their ploys even just once, you encourage that meltdown to be a rewarding resolution every time, for they know that if they break you down hard enough, you will submit to their rule.

In no circumstance does this mean you should allow your child to harm themselves or someone else as you position your point across that they will not get their way, especially for poor behavior. However, you should not be afraid to let them cry or sort it out themselves, either. Let your child sit in their room and sort their emotions out for themselves. It may feel painful or overwhelming to you as their parent, but understand that this is an important part of your child learning emotional self-regulation. Even though your child's ability to regulate their emotions may be inhibited, it does not mean it is entirely ruined. While your child's emotional dysregulation may differ to a neurotypical individual, a child with a behavioral disorder still grasps the capacity to regulate themselves, and it is crucial that they discover their own unique way of doing so. Help your child by providing a safe space to regulate within as they learn how to cope and manage their emotions.

Course Correct With Yourself, First

If you find yourself amid a meltdown and cannot seem to position yourself or your child back on track, you need to stop and recall the importance of putting your own safety mask on, first. Before you can help your child regulate themselves and steer away from intensifying outbursts, you have to address your own emotional state. Reflect on your present thoughts while attempting to calm yourself down. Take a deep breath. Children, no matter what age, will always heighten to match their parents escalated state. This means if you are yelling, screaming, crying, or arguing with your child, you are inadvertently encouraging them to escalate their own behavior, to match yours. If you have committed the mistake of engaging into dispute, or if your own anguish is causing heightened distress for your child, you need to stop and walk away from the situation. Relax your entire body and mind for a few moments while you compose yourself back into a grounded, calm state. Then, with a compassionate and peaceful approach, you are able to support your child in achieving the same sense of tranquility.

Upon recognizing the increasingly intensifying outburst, peacefully inform your child that you are walking away from this environment for a few minutes so you can calm yourself and address the situation in a more composed and productive manner. If possible, leave your child in a safe space such as their bedroom and have them wait there until you are ready to address the situation in a more respectful fashion.

Then, as you stated remove yourself from the area and start the process of calming yourself down.

An excellent way to calm yourself down is to use a square breath. This breathing rhythm will help you calm your emotions quickly, bring peace back to your mind and body, and prepare you for reconciling this troubling situation with your child. To begin, inhale through your nose for a count of four, hold at the top of the breathe for another count of four, then calmly exhale through your mouth for a count of four, at the bottom of the breath, hold for a final count of four. Repeat this breathing pattern at least 10 times before presenting yourself a moment to collect your thoughts. Subsequently, review your behavioral plan, determine what course of action to take, and return to your child in a calmer manner, ready to take action per your behavioral plan. Even if you have already deviated from the plan, you can always realign back on track at any point. This shows your child that, despite the mistake you made by letting the situation get out of control once again, you are serious about using this new method of approach, and you will uphold it through thick and thin.

A child with a behavioral disorder like oppositional defiant disorder (ODD) will likely attempt to throw back in your face the fact that you already deviated away from the original behavioral plan. They may challenge your rationale with the use of guilt, embarrassment, or shame as a way to encourage you to feel deplorable about the deviancy from the plan. The child will push fairly hard at this to pressure and manipulate you to reach their preferred outcome and get their way. You need to be aware of their tricks and prevent them from doing so by standing firm in your behavioral plan. Know that you are on the right track and that even if you had to course correct, you are making far more progress than you had in the past. Once you are done dealing with that particular situation, be sure to celebrate your success of rearranging things back on track, and give yourself the opportunity to release any undesirable emotions you may be holding onto. If you have someone you tend to talk to when things get out of control with your child or someone who is helping you improve the situation, now would be a great time to reach out to that person so you can obtain assistance. The calmer you become following a meltdown or a mistake, and the more perspective you accumulate, the easier it will be for you to view it as a positive experience regardless of what your child may have said. This way, you can go into the next experience with even more courage and confidence, and a greater ability to keep things from derailing. Please don't take what your child says to heart too much, understand they are just words and are being used in an attempt to assume control. You are doing great despite what anyone says. Over time, you and your child will be experiencing a far less dramatic approach to discipline and household rules!

Chapter Five:

Diffusing Defiance and Conflict

No matter how effective your new no-drama disciplinary measures may be, it is inevitable that defiance and conflict will arise at some point in time. Even if you enforce your new found knowledge with expert precision, these issues will surface because your child's response has become as habitual as your own. Just as you habitually respond with stress, exasperation, or frustration any time your child is about to erupt, your child habitually responds with an explosion any time their trigger is pulled. Regardless of what the trigger is, the response to it comes as naturally as breathing, which is why it is so instant and intense. Each time the reaction is repeated, it becomes stronger and more impulsive, making it more challenging for you and your child to get a handle on it and prevent it from worsening over time. As frustrating as that may sound, remember that it is rooted in their past experiences, and it is up to you to educate them how to appropriately "reconfigure" their minds, so these habitual responses change. It may take time for them to shift entirely, but with consistency and practice, they *will* shift. You just have to remain patient and persistent.

Diffusing defiance and conflict is something that can be done before a conflicting moment arises, or after it has already commenced. As soon as you see the opportunity for habitual defiance or conflict to arise, you want to create space for you to diffuse and navigate it in a more positive manner with your child. The idea is that if you can prevent the defiant outburst from reaching the point of needing disciplinary action, you can generate the ultimate no-drama approach because there is truly nothing for you to punish. When there is nothing to discipline, there is no fear of a major meltdown arising due to the experience of disciplinary action.

It is important that, in taking this approach, you do *not* attempt to avoid conflict altogether. Instead, you want to reach the point of facing previously triggering experiences head-on gradually without the trigger actually being pulled. If you can teach your child to diffuse themselves, you can face these engagements without such a drastic conflict taking place.

Remaining Patient in the Moment

Before you can expect your child to practice a less intense behavior, you need to learn how to cultivate less intense behavior yourself. You can do this by being patient with yourself and your child, and modeling the type of behavior that you want your child to express, also. When you model patience for your child, ensure that you are vocal about the patience you are modeling, as this helps your child understand what you are doing and ensures they are actually bearing witness to the behavior you are modeling. While your child will inevitably notice a difference in your attitude when you express patience, if you do not clearly describe what you are doing, they might not clearly understand what you are doing, or why. This is especially true if you do not typically model patient behavior when your child is having a difficult time.

Forming a sense of patience for yourself in any present moment stems from understanding the entirety of the situation and preparing yourself for it in advance. Each day, prepare for the fact that you and your child will inevitably have a few challenging experiences, and create a productive mindset ahead of time that enables you through those challenges. This way, when you inevitably reach them, you are already at a point of understanding and patience in your mind, which means you are more likely to respond in such a manner, too.

The best way to express patience for your child is to acknowledge what is currently happening whilst advising them that you are going to take a moment to breathe before you address the situation. During this breath, you are being patient with yourself and the moment and creating a sense of peace around yourself, so you can address the situation more productively and respectfully. To your child, you might say something like, "I am going to take a moment to breathe, because I can see that this is a troubling situation and neither of us are feeling good about it. In doing so, I can invite more patience while we learn to navigate this better." Of course, adjust your language to match your child's age and coherency, so they clearly understand what you have said.

Promoting a Problem-Solving Experience

After you have created space for patience and taken a moment for yourself, you need to promote an aptitude for problem-solving. This requires both you and your child to share interactions and conversation that promote a problem-solving environment. When you are both able to connect into a similar frame of mind and create a desire to solve the problem you are facing, it minimizes imminent outbursts while maximizing resolutions because you are able to address these situations head-on, together. This mindset is far more productive than any alternative, offering the greatest opportunity for you both to explore the situation in a positive, thorough manner. A major benefit of this approach to resolving problems is that you show your child that you are on their team and that you desire to find a solution together. When your child realizes they can rely on you and that you are insistent on helping them, rather than hindering them, they are likely to be more receptive to your approach.

Internally, focusing on problem-solving takes you out of the mindset of "what is wrong with us?" or "what is wrong with my child?" and allows you to instead focus on what can be done to form greater harmony in that moment. When you alternate your mindset, it becomes easier for you to lead yourself and your child into a more positive, productive atmosphere.

Within your child, focusing on problem-solving not only takes their attention off the trigger, but it also teaches them how to solve problems they may face in their lives. It is a common misconception that children with behavioral disorders are incapable of regulating themselves or solving their own problems. They, like any child, are fully capable, however the method in which they approach these skills or the amount of time it takes to successfully regulate themselves may differ. Teaching your child how to problem-solve using their own unique reasoning, logic, and skills ensure that when they arrive at troubling situations, they have healthier coping methods for those situations. In the end, this proves to be a profound life experience for your child.

The Solution Starts With You

Shifting into a problem-solving mode of thinking starts with you. As always, you need to be modeling productive and positive behavior. Your child will look up to you as a role model, absorbing your processes as they develop and learning how to regulate and care for themselves in the long run based on their external experiences. Your own problem-solving should focus on three specific points of the problem: why the problem occurred, how the problem is affecting your child, and how the problem is affecting you.

In addressing why the complication occurred, you need to focus your problem-solving skills toward how you can avoid this setback from happening again in the future. Remember, this does not mean avoiding the situation altogether; rather, it means learning how to cope with the situation so that the trigger itself is less intense if it is to reignite. As the parent, you need to decide how you will teach your child effective coping mechanisms so they can live through that situation without such challenging behaviors being triggered as a result.

Take the time to reflect on why that problem transpired, understand what is going through your child's mind, and why they are having such a troubling time with this challenge. Understanding these prerequisites allows you to provide a deeper sense of compassion for your child, and an enhanced capacity to choose an appropriate course of action. Now is a great time to incorporate your child into the problem-solving experience, and to discuss possible outcomes with them in a way that matches their conversational abilities. Together you can construct a solution that supports their needs in calming down and how you can best diffuse the situation in the future.

Lastly, you need to address how the problem affected you as the parent. Understanding how and why your own emotions were triggered, and what made that particular challenge so difficult for you to navigate. You may also unravel opportunities for improving your approach, facilitating a greater ability to diffuse defiance and conflict in future circumstances.

Genuinely Listening to Your Child's Needs

Children who experience defiant rages and intense meltdowns often struggle with the ability to control themselves because they do not adequately grasp what is going on internally. Their lack of understanding and inability to define those emotions impedes on their capacity to appropriately express how they truly feel.

Actively listening to your child will welcome two refreshing benefits. The first benefit is that your child feels heard, and as an influence of feeling heard, you help them feel accepted. This state of acceptance demonstrates that they are irrefutably surrounded by people that care for them. Furthermore, providing a safe environment to articulate and express their emotions. Another advantage to taking in your child's input is that you are able to clearly understand how they are feeling, which means you can help your child correctly label their feelings and express those feelings in a more productive manner. For example, if your child is feeling irritated because things did not go their way, you can help them describe these feelings and recognize these feelings as being natural and safe to feel. You can also help them understand a more effective way of resolving those feelings of anger so they can completely express them without creating feelings of frustration, embarrassment, shame, or otherwise.

Genuinely listening to your child and his or her wishes is a eloquent means to quickly diffuse any situation, yet it is a commonly skipped step. It is a challenging, yet important initiative to remind yourself to slow down and listen when your own emotions running high. Patience is key here, as it encourages you to calm down and take the time to understand what your child is upset about. Once you have heard exactly what your child has to say, you can take relevant action to effectively diffuse the situation and move on in a more appropriate manner.

Practicing the Redirection

An exceptional method for diffusing defiance and conflict rapidly is called redirection. When you redirect your child's focus, you are essentially breaking their attention away from one thing and guiding it toward something more positive. Turning their attention away from a trigger and toward a solution is an excellent example of a redirection, though it can be achieved in many other ways, too.

If your child has a tendency to habitually respond to certain triggers in an overwhelming manner, now is an excellent opportunity to practice redirecting their attention before the explosive outburst toward a peaceful outcome. Learning to correctly perform this particular redirect will affect your child's habitual response into a more productive process, effectively diffusing any conflict before it arises.

For example, let's say putting your child's shoes on so you can leave the house is a common point of conflict, and every time you ask them to put their shoes on they are triggered. You may notice that you tend to state the need to put their shoes on as follows: "Can you please put your shoes on so we can go grocery shopping?" At this point, you have already lost your child's attention at the point of asking them to put their shoes on, and they have begun melting down before you even finished your sentence. Instead, you might say, "We need to go buy some more of your favorite snacks so you can have them to eat for school! Put your shoes on so we can go. [Hand them their shoes.] What flavor will you pick this time?" Following the second example, you emphasize focus on the benefit they are getting from going out and minimizing the stress of putting their shoes on. As long as you keep them distracted and sell them on the benefits of going out, it is likely that they will put their shoes on quickly so they can enjoy the aforementioned benefits.

You can perform this sort of redirection in absolutely any situation you find yourself in with your child, regardless of the subject of that situation. In order for it to be productive, though, you need to know what your child does not want to do, and what they do want to do. Structure your delivery by selling them on the benefit of getting to do what they want to do before asking them about what they tend to be triggered by. In turn, you maintain their positive attention, and they are more likely to comply.

If you find yourself in a situation where a meltdown has been instigated, and you have already put the request out there, the best thing you can do is practice patience and begin the redirection mid-conversation. Stop nagging your child or asking them about the undesirable activity for a while and focus on the more desirable action until you have their positive interest. *Afterward*, implement the undesirable activity back into the mix. This system of redirection should enable you to rapidly diffuse conflicts and realign yourself back into a positive solution-oriented experience with your child.

Chapter Six:

Changing Your Parenting Approach

If you wish to introduce a truly profound transformation, you must adjust your parenting style to accommodate. Creating fundamental reform in your parenting approach ensures that you are enforcing a robust long-term outlook that will suit the needs of your child and propel you both toward a more peaceful experience overall.

The nurturing style you develop for your child is not much different from one that a parent of a child without behavioral disorders would create. However, your findings regarding what you need to do and how you need to address certain situations will likely differ from parents with neurotypical children. It is important that you take your parenting seriously and stay true to your processes, and in time you *will* see drastic improvements to your quality of life. Likewise, the affirmative attention concentrated toward your child will inspire an uplifting, wholesome relationship together. This healthy association encourages any inclinations by your child to please you or listen to your direction, rather than ignore your presence or assume that you will not support them in protecting their happiness and wellbeing.

Developing a parenting style that works in favor of you and your child can be difficult. To support your growth and help design your perfect parenting style, I have listed ten steps below entailing the fundamentals for you to build upon. Your style will certainly change over time as your child's needs advance, and your understanding of how to meet their needs develops. However, if you can use these ten steps to create a basic parenting style that you can follow for now, the style can be evolved over time to become even more productive.

Step One: Listen

Your child, like any child, knows exactly what they want. They recognize their likes and dislikes, and understand what does and does not work for them. Children are incredible at understanding themselves and following their inner compass, so long as their parents allow them to.

Before you define any parenting style, listen to your child, and respect their wishes. Acknowledge what they have to say, and ensure that they are aware of the fact that you have heard and understood their needs. If your child is unwilling or unable to communicate clearly, you can read in to what they are expressing through their actions and behaviors. For example, big meltdowns indicate that they are displeased with something and that it is not working for them. This is a great opportunity for you to start adapting your parenting style.

Step Two: Be Respectful

Your children deserve your respect at all times, this includes any time disciplining your child, creating rules, or setting boundaries. There are many excellent practices that can guide a child toward positive, preferred behavior without treating them in a way that is humiliating or degrading in any shape or form. A great example would be the redirection method as previously described, or to sit down and have a discussion with them at a later time to reflect upon their recent behavior. Often, taking the time to dissect a situation and discuss your expectations in a language your child can understand is plenty to help them feel optimistic about their ability to make meaningful changes in their behavior. At times, you may need to encourage multiple discussions with your child to effectively reach the desired resolution. Just as you would prefer someone explain your faults or inappropriate behaviors to you, you need to replicate the same belief to your child, as many times as it may take. Your child deserves those gentle considerations, rather than to find themselves being disciplined with harsh language, yelling, or other dramatic means.

Step Three: Model Positive Behavior

Your children need to see you modeling ideal behavior, making smart choices, resolving your oversights, and owning up to your faults. When you model positive behavior for your children in as many forms as possible, you enable your children to see exactly how they should be dealing with each of their own issues, too. While it may be challenging to model positive behavior for your children at times, it is important to be mindful of the fact that they are always looking up to you, and they always demand your guidance. When it comes to children with behavioral disorders, it may seem like your behavior does not entirely matter because they do not mimic your affirmative action or choose to behave independently on their own anyway. This is just absolutely untrue. Every child needs a positive, meaningful role model to inspire them to do their best. However, we are all individuals and in turn all have our own specific characteristics and that's okay, were not clones so you must respect some aspects of your child's personality may never mirror yours. While they may not be able to follow along perfectly, your positive behavior undeniably aids them in doing the best they can. Additionally, it becomes easier to encourage improved behavior when you are acting in integrity with what you are asking of them, especially children who experience behavioral disorders and who may use your lack of integrity against you, such as with ODD.

Step Four: Give Your Child Choices

Choices provide your child with the opportunity to feel as though they have some degree of control over their lives, and it teaches them how to use that control in a positive regard. When you provide your child choices, you are treating them with respect, trusting them to make decisions, and teaching them about independence. You should adjust your range of choices to match your child's level of need, as well as their level of understanding, to ensure that you are offering them choices that empower them, rather than overwhelm them. You could invite your child to choose which shoes to wear, which toy they want to play with, or which grocery store they want to shop at. These simple choices do not have a big impact on your ability to fulfill your obligations, but they have a major impact on your child's ability to cooperate. As you listen to your child and pay attention to their needs, it will become easier to determine which choices they can manage, and which choices should wait until they gain the aptitude to succeed. After you give your child a choice, always be available to support them in navigating those choices or making decisions if they need it.

Step Five: Be Clear About Your Expectations

Clear expectations are a necessity, particularly concerning a child with a behavioral disorder. Being well-defined about your expectations of your child helps them have total awareness of what is expected of them, so they know how to make appropriate choices at various points throughout each activity. A great way to be clear about your expectations is to sit your child down and discuss your expectations before you do something. For example, if you are going to a birthday party for another child, you might discuss your expectations of your child regarding what needs to happen before, during, and after the birthday party. Try to keep it simple, and with as few limitations as possible; otherwise, it may become overwhelming for your child. You might say something along the lines of, "I need you to bathe and dress before we leave, listen to the rules when we are there, and leave the party without arguing at exactly four o'clock." It may also be advantageous to have your child repeat these expectations back to you so they have fully internalized the expectations you have of them.

Step Six: Establish Clear Rules

In addition to expectations set for individual experiences, it can be helpful to establish clear rules. Clear rules, as we previously discussed, should be standard rules that apply in every situation. To remind you, excellent rules would include: being respectful, doing as you are asked, refraining from arguing, and completing your chores in a timely manner.

Step Seven: Use Praise Correctly

Children thrive on positive praise. Negative attention, such as discipline, can become a slippery slope with children as they tend to make many mistakes and do not always grasp the awareness they need to make better choices. If you are always disciplining your child for their choices, they may start to believe that the only attention they can possibly receive is bad attention, and that is not healthy for a child's mental wellness. Eventually, they may start to seek out negative attention because they have become accustomed to it. Furthermore, your child may start to make poor choices more purposefully, in an effort to gain your attention. Alternatively, some children may respond by having increasingly lowlier responses to the discipline, while continuing to lack the necessary knowledge to stop making the same mistake over and over again. Save discipline for particularly serious situations and opt instead to shape your child's behavior using positive praise. Every time your child does something you appreciate, pay close attention, and celebrate them for their choices, while encouraging them to perform more of these positive actions. When your child does something you do not like, ignore it unless you absolutely have to discipline them because it is particularly wrong. By emphasizing positive reinforcement over negative discipline, you create a parenting style that encourages your child in a positive, compassionate manner.

Step Eight: Plan Ahead

Planning ahead is a necessity for any parent, but especially parents with children who may be likely to have intense responses to seemingly standard stimuli. If your child tends to have major meltdowns when they are exposed to stress, for example, and you know they will soon be exposed to a stressful situation, you need to plan ahead for how you will navigate that specific situation.

The simplest way to plan ahead is to keep a schedule and pay attention to the tasks that need to be completed on a day to day basis. Each evening or on the morning of, plan for the day ahead and decide how you will make that day as stress-free as possible ahead of time. This way, when you are actively moving through the day and achieving your necessary tasks, you are not caught unprepared in a challenging situation. This practice will also assist your own stress levels as you have already mentally prepared for any forthcoming stressful experiences.

Step Nine: Follow Through

Parents of children with behavioral disorders tend to report that it feels more challenging to follow through with consequences than it does for parents of children who are neurotypical. You might feel like it is cruel or unkind to follow through with consequences because your child is already dealing with so much, and on some level, you feel guilty that they face the unique challenges they do. While it is perfectly understandable to feel guilt and grief around your child's troubling experiences in life, it is important to understand that *not* following through on consequences is worse than delivering them in the first place. Your child needs to have well-defined regulation, and the assurance that consequences if they fail to do as they have been asked will be followed through with, *assuming* that the expectations they were told to meet were reasonable for their abilities. If they were, then following through on consequences teaches your child to hold themselves accountable, take responsibility for their actions, and complete the tasks that are expected of them. Not following through teaches your child to take advantage of and manipulate others or disregard others' needs or opinions because they will get away with not listening, or performing tasks required of them. You must follow through, respectfully and compassionately, on the consequences that were promised to your child if they decide not to respect what you have asked of them.

Step Ten: Be Consistent

Lastly, consistency is essential. Children with behavioral disorders will struggle in circumstances that lack consistency and regularity because they find themselves experiencing extreme confusion around what is expected of them and what will happen if they do not fulfill those expectations. You need to ensure that the guidelines, and the consequences of not following those guidelines, all remain consistent if your child is to thrive. With that in mind, you should be mindful of the extreme need for consistency and never make rules, set expectations, or promise a specific set of consequences if you are not ready to follow through with them. Take some time to think about specific guidelines that need to be followed, and define a set of expectations that can reasonably be followed in just about any set of circumstances. This way, every time you remind your child of the rules or set expectations, they are consistent, and your child knows what to expect and can rely on things to be roughly the same in every situation. The same goes for consequences: define consequences in advance that would be reasonable to any situation, and practice following through on the same consequences every single time. In turn, your child comes to expect them and knows how to act if they wish to avoid the consequences.

Chapter Seven:

Maintaining a Peaceful Environment

A s you focus on crafting more productive ways of navigating difficult parenting experiences, it is important that you also prioritize creating a peaceful environment for yourself and your family. A peaceful environment is essential to your family, as it enables you all to thrive in a safe, comfortable space that nourishes your wellbeing.

To form a peaceful atmosphere, you need to establish a setting that avoids yelling, angry outbursts, antagonizing acts, disrespectful behaviors, or other forms of defiance or conflict. This may seem impossible if you have a child who routinely acts out, whether purposefully or at random, it still remains necessary. This peaceful environment does not guarantee that you will not have falling outs, but it does ensure that you have plenty of peace in between meltdowns to ensure everyone returns to a state of calm.

When you do not possess an adequate amount of time to return to a sense of calm between outbursts, meltdowns tend to trigger more frequently. This is because, rather than having the opportunity to fully break out of your fight or flight response and resume your state of rest or digest, you constantly remain on edge. Though this heightened state, you and your child are more prone to flare-ups.

There are plenty of habits to encourage a more passive atmosphere in your home while simultaneously decreasing the amount of defiance and conflict you experience with your child. By exercising a few simple concepts, you can create an environment that feels more like a haven, and less like a place of stress and trauma for everyone involved.

Discourage Yelling in the Home

While yelling across the house may seem like an easier way to get your child's attention than, say, walking over to their room and talking to them, this can actually foster an increasingly stressful environment. Yelling through the door or wall at your child, or allowing them to yell at you this way, can set the tone for meltdowns rather quickly. During the yelling process, everyone is already elevating their energy through the simple act of shouting. Further, miscommunications are far more likely under these circumstances, and that can make for even larger meltdowns if you are not careful.

Rather than welcoming screaming as a means of communication, set a rule that everyone must speak within close enough proximity that you can converse with a calm voice. This means no more yelling across the house or through walls to communicate. Instead, you can either walk to each other and start talking or knock on a bedroom door and wait to be invited in before you start talking to each other. This way, yelling is discouraged, and peaceful, respectful communication is encouraged instead. A little more effort is required for this strategy as you will need to consistently close the gap between each other before communication can commence. The tradeoff however is astounding and removes a lot of tension in the air.

Create Safe Spaces for Everyone

When chaos ensues, it can become extremely stressful for everyone living under the same roof, even those not directly involved in the chaos. Chaos may not always consist of outbursts of anger or emotional meltdowns, but may instead be a challenging moment or a particularly difficult day filled with challenging sensations. Having a designated safe space for everyone in the home ensures that everyone has their own area to retreat to if things become overwhelming. For your child, their bedroom might become their safe space. For you, your safe space may be your bedroom, office, or even the bathroom, so you can have a bath as you relax and unwind. Regardless of where they are, safe spaces should always be respected, and anytime someone is in their safe space, people should be particularly gentle and kind to that person as a way to show respect while they practice regulating their emotions.

It is important that you recall the value of modeling positive behavior for your children and that, in the process of creating safe spaces, you actually use yours. When you are angry or upset, let your child know you are retreating to your safe space so you can calm down and regulate your emotions, and genuinely follow through in doing so. Let them see you in your safe space, taking deep breaths, releasing your emotions, and helping yourself adjust back to a state of calm. This way, when they go to use their safe space (or are encouraged to use it during a meltdown,) they have an example of what they should do with their time there to help them come back to a state of calm and peace. This can include practicing meditation, mindfulness, breathing routines, soothing activities like drawing or journaling to name a few.

Follow the Same Routine Every Day

Routines may seem like a dreadful way to spend your day, especially if you tend to be the type of person who does things spontaneously or who dislikes planning too far in advance. However, routines are important for children, especially those who require clear expectations and consistency to aid them with their self-regulation and emotional wellbeing.

Set up a routine for yourself and your child that you can follow every day, even on days off, and be sure to follow it. If you create a fun, easy-to-follow routine, it becomes enjoyable for your entire family to follow that routine, and you experience even more benefit from your routine. Since you need a routine that you can follow each day, it may be ideal to have a morning, afternoon, and bedtime routine that can be followed, while leaving room for adaptations during the rest of the day. This way, you can accommodate for the fact that things like school, work, errands, and leisurely tasks are often rotated during the daytime hours. You can also create routines around how specific tasks are done, such as getting ready for school or preparing to go out for leisurely activities, as this can help psychologically prepare your child for these activities, too.

Unplug on a Regular Basis

Studies have shown that excessive screen time or interaction with devices can increase behavioral issues in neurotypical children and adults, and can have an extremely detrimental impact on the wellbeing of children with behavioral disorders. Regularly unplugging your entire family from technology is an important approach to create more peace in your home by eliminating a known trigger from your lives.

Aside from assisting with behavioral and emotional regulation, unplugging on a regular basis ensures that you have plenty of quality time to spend with your family. In regards to screen time, implementing a time limit, or allowing time after chores, homework or other important tasks have been completed can be a healthy guideline to employ. As human beings we are becoming more and more intimate with technology as we further advance, I just want to mention this as a lot of parents consider technology to be the "devil". Consider that time has changed since your upbringing and kids of today can benefit exponentially from learning various technological skills.

Express Gratitude on a Regular Basis

Expressing gratitude for each other and the life you are blessed with is an excellent way to improve the quality of your relationships. Just as positive praise regularly encourages children to behave in a more positive manner, hearing that you are grateful for their existence or that you are appreciative to experience the present moment with them improves the quality of positive connections they share with you, too. As you continue to increase this positivity, your child begins to welcome a more peaceful association with the outside world and will gain a greater initiative to work toward more positive growth and change in their lives.

Do Things Together As a Family

Life can get hectic, and making time for your family can be challenging. Nevertheless, family time is crucial. Neurodivergent children thrive on structure and connection, and they tend to do better when they know that they can trust and rely on their family. Taking the time to do things together as a family ensures that your child feels a sense of peace and strong foundation within their family unit. It also creates the opportunity for your entire family to appreciate fun times together, which increases your bond and encourages a tranquil, compassionate atmosphere within your household.

Partaking in activities that are enjoyable for everyone involved is important to note. You should be mindful of anything that may trigger your child to avoid creating an overwhelming environment. Your plans may not always consist of extravagant trips to carnivals and movie theatres, so consider planning ahead before even the simplest of activities such as; playing board games, growing your own herb garden, kicking the football, baking a cake together, or even going for a walk at a nearby park. Do what works for your family, and create space for your child to feel safe and comfortable. This time should not be about expanding their comfort zone or coping skills, but about enjoying a positive, peaceful time together as a family.

Maintain Composure with Mistakes

Mistakes or oversights are inevitable, no matter how hard you try to avoid them. Remaining composed through any of those slipups is an important aspect of maintaining peace, as it gives you the flexibility to navigate any upheavals with a calm and collected mindset. You might have noticed that, in the past, anytime a mistake presented itself, it seemed to spiral, and the day grew more and more stressful as time went by. This is because after one mistake was made, you remained on edge, expecting more problems to come out of that experience, and in turn more chaos erupted.

When you perceive mistakes with a sense of grace, you deal with the mistake, and trust that it was an isolated experience. Rather than anticipating further misfortune or bracing yourself for more chaos, you regain composure and work toward maintaining peace. As a result, you welcome a shift in perspective, and any upcoming obstacles can be faced with a relaxed state of calm and clarity.

Chapter Eight:

A 3 Step Process for Getting Things Done

Many parents of children who have behavioral disorders find that it takes an exceptional amount of time to get anything done. It may feel like you are constantly arguing with your child or cautiously avoiding meltdowns, to the point where it starts to consume other aspects of life. Whether it is grocery shopping, leaving for school, cleaning the house, or various other daily activities, you need to cultivate a sure-fire system to get your child on board and start freeing up your time.

Rest assured, there are plenty of time-efficient methods that you can implement to hastily complete those tasks. The easiest way is to follow this 3 step process for getting things done, although it may not *feel* easy at first. As you continue to enforce this routine, it will become habitual and will make the entire process of completing tasks far easier for you and your child. Before you know it, you will be finishing everything on your to-do list faster than ever before!

Step 1: Prepare for What Needs to Be Done

The three step process is best if you visualize it as being a container that you are creating to hold space for a positive experience with your child. The first step of building the container is building the foundation. The basis of this foundation is formed by preparing yourself for what needs to be achieved and formulating how you can develop the most successful and peaceful experience. At this stage, you are not focused on anything to do with your child; instead, you are focused on creating a solid foundation for yourself.

Knowing that your own mental and emotional needs are cared for and that you have planned our own essential wellbeing *first* ensures that you feel confident in your ability to get through the upcoming task regardless of what happens. This important preparation ensures that you are far more calm, peaceful, and stable going into the experience, which means your child will be more likely to have a similar experience. When your child has someone grounded and level-headed guiding them, it becomes easier for them to imitate a more peaceful experience, too.

Step 2: Prepare Your Child for What Needs to be Done

Next, you need to prepare your child for what needs to be done. This step is similar to preparing yourself, except you will be guiding your child through a similar process you undertook. You can start by clearly defining what needs to happen and setting expectations for your child so they familiarize with what is expected of them. It is especially helpful to prepare your child with an escape route, should they feel they need one. For example, if they are in the grocery store and begin to experience intense and overwhelming emotions, clearly explain how they can communicate this to you in their own way so you can help them overcome their struggle. Rather than having them escalate to the point of total meltdown, you can teach your child how they can prevent it from happening beforehand or at least minimizing the outburst.

If your child is particularly overwhelmed by participating in activities, it may be helpful to plan yourself into their plan for escape. For instance, you may set the expectation that every 10-20 minutes, you will ask your child how they are coping, and they can whisper a reply of "bad," a codeword, or tightly squeeze your hand if they are not thriving in this environment. If they are managing ok, they can claim they are in fact "good" or hold your hand loosely to let you know they are okay. This type of preparation is a wonderful way to help your child feel more emotionally supported and safe, which means they will be more likely to have a positive experience when going out. Often, breaking the experience down into bite-sized pieces and preparing your child for those experiences is plenty to prepare them for the time ahead. From there, you can focus on getting through just one part at a time until you have seen the entire task through.

Step 3: Do It

Lastly, you need to follow through on exactly what you have prepared for. Taking action on the necessary steps for taking care of yourself and your child as you get through any proposed task. When you perform the appropriate measures, you cultivate a less stressful experience by nurturing both of your emotional needs. Further, you teach your child how to take care of themselves during troubling or overwhelming experiences so that, in the future, they can hopefully navigate these experiences with greater success, too.

It is very important that you follow the exact expectations you set for your child during the process of completing this task, even if things around you start to go out of sorts. Your child learns that they can rely on your guidance and trust in what you tell them. Over time this entire process will become easier and easier as you build a stronger understanding of each other's needs.

Chapter Nine:

From Punishment to Rewards

Punishing your child is an ineffective means of realizing objectives. When you chastise your child, you create a negative environment that is intended to inhibit unwanted actions, however you simultaneously create overwhelming emotional responses such as embarrassment, shame, and guilt. Likewise, once you develop the tendency to punish your child, you have allowed the unwanted behavior to foster beyond control. By now, you are so frustrated with the behavior that you explode bellicosely toward the origin, which generates a burst of frustration and a belligerent encounter ensues. The trouble with prolonged punishment is that it teaches your child over time that unless someone is openly screaming at them, they are not in need of changing their behavior. Unfortunately, this habit develops into adulthood, and before they realize that a change in behavior is necessary they seek to be yelled at or to drive people to the point of irritability. This is extremely inhibiting to their ability to cultivate healthy relationships with others.

Rather than punishing your child, you need to focus on praising them more frequently. You need to set them up for success by encouraging them to partake in experiences that gift them praise, and discouraging them from partaking in the experiences that would typically cause punishment. Building a healthy environment, so your child is more likely to participate in things you want them to do, and less likely to do the things you don't want them to, is an excellent way to promote good behavior.

Empathize With Your Child

When your child begins to experience an overwhelming amount of emotions, their fight or flight response will kick in, and their entire system will be overloaded with adrenaline. At this point, they cannot completely comprehend foreign concepts because their brain has altered to a defensive state, not a receptive state. Instead of punishing your child for their bad behavior, it's time to help them escape that fight or flight response so that they may reach a state of calm. Their brain will return back to a more receptive state and allow your now teachable child to comprehend any guidance and lessons you may explain to them.

Letting your child know that you understand their feelings and offer compassion for what they are going through creates a safe atmosphere for them to work through and regulate those emotions. Once your child has eased their emotions, your child will feel far better, and so will you. At that point, you can discuss what those emotions were and how they can better be managed in the future.

Support Their Learning Experience

Children *crave* learning, and when they are in an environment that supports their ability to learn, they thrive. It is important to remember that your child cannot learn exclusively through being told what to do; but also shown through demonstration and regularity. A great way to understand this is to reflect back to potty training, or tying their shoelaces. Initially, you were highly engaged in the process, demonstrating to your child what to do and how to do it, and encouraging them to follow your guidance. Over time, you backed off until without your support they were able complete these tasks on their own. The same methodology applies to all areas of their growth.

When your child advances to a point where they are ready to learn something new, your support is vital. Be as hands-on as required to teach your child how to navigate that particular experience in a positive manner, then start slowly letting them gain their independence as they familiarize with the new concept. Support your child in upholding good choices and seeking positive experiences, and are teach them how to receive positive feedback for the actions they take.

Connection Before Correction

When a child has misbehaved, it may be due to a troubling emotion that drove their bad behavior. For example, if your child is hitting another child, it is because they have experienced an emotion that has made them feel angry enough to smack them. Their inability to regulate or cope with that emotion is what lead to their bad behavior; it was not spontaneous in nature.

Taking the time to connect with your child by hugging them and affirming that you love them before you begin correcting their behavior ensures that they receive the support they require to navigate their troubling emotions, first. You can then discuss what was wrong with their behavior and educate them on a more positive means for dealing with their emotions in the future.

Set Limits in a Loving Way

Punishment is typically used as a means of setting limits, though it is often allotted in a negative or critical fashion. Learning to set limits in an affectionate manner allows you to acknowledge and correct negative behavior without exploding into rages of anger or otherwise experiencing an undesirably emotional outburst with your child. For instance, let's imagine that your child wants to keep playing their game instead of getting ready for bed, so they start having a meltdown or show the early stages of an emotional outburst due to their desire to keep playing. Rather than retorting with "Too bad" or "It's time for bed, so stop playing, NOW!" you might try something along the lines of: "Wow you're really enjoying this game aren't you! I understand it's hard to stop playing and get ready for bed. Let's continue with this game tomorrow." This way, you are acknowledging your child's feelings, having empathy for them, and still upholding the limits so you can encourage your child to do as they have been asked.

If it is possible, at a point where you are setting limits, you can also incorporate a redirection to encourage your child to make a better decision on their own. For example, you might say: "I know it's hard to stop playing and get ready for bed. Would you like to brush your teeth first, or get into your pajamas first?" Again, this acknowledges their feelings and desires, yet still makes it clear that action needs to be taken.

Teach Your Kid to Fix Their Mistakes

Making mistakes is an inevitable part of life, but children may be more prone to them, considering they have not learned from many of their own mistakes in the past. Further, they have not had the opportunity to properly learn how to adapt and navigate their mistakes, either. Teaching your child how to address and remedy their mistakes ensures they recognize how to overcome any potential adversities, and in turn, more likely to navigate them in a peaceful manner.

When it comes to teaching your child how to navigate mistakes, always do so in a matter-of-fact way. Do not make a big deal about the mistake, as doing so can trigger a huge emotional response, and that can make dealing with the mistake far more challenging. Instead, acknowledge that a mistake happened and focus on fixing the mistake with your child, so they realize mistakes are not worth a major emotional outcry, and that they can easily be resolved and worked out.

Use the Word "Yes" More Often

A great way to encourage your child to follow your guidance is to use the word "yes" more often. The more you can say yes, the more likely your child will be to listen because they feel a positive association with the word itself.

For example, if you exclaim "No, you cannot keep playing because you need to go to bed," or "No you cannot do that you need to get dressed," you are advocating the word "no" *a lot.* Your child perpetually hears every "no" and grows increasingly frustrated with each one, initiating a decline in receptivity toward you. Instead, you could insist; "Yes, it is time for bed, I'd love for you to show me your game tomorrow?" Or "Yes, you can absolutely do that after you get dressed." Or "Yes, I love you, and I am so lucky to be your parent. YES!" This type of affirmative response encourages positive emotions within your child, which inspires a far more likely inclination to listen and do what you have asked them to do.

Build Your Relationship Daily

Part of creating the opportunity for your child to listen to you is to build upon your relationship with them every single day, as the more positive they feel around you, the more likely they will be to listen to your guidance. You can influence your relationship with your child by spending time together, talking about their interests, participating in things they are interested in, and spending time laughing together. The activity itself is of little concern, if your child wishes to play video games with you, accept this invitation and have them teach you how to play alongside them. The purpose is to share quality time together. Make jokes, partake in things they enjoy, and generally have a good time together. The more you laugh together, the stronger your relationship becomes, and the more likely you will be to enjoy your relationship with your child. This positive attention also makes them feel safer and more trusting in you, which makes it easier for them to navigate their emotions around you. As that transformation transpires, you can teach them how to navigate their emotions in general, which helps them thrive away from you, too.

It is a good idea to schedule at least 20 minutes per day to invest in quality time with your child. For these 20 minutes, do not touch your phone or engage in distractions, instead just focus solely on your child and an activity you can do together. On a regular basis, such as weekly or every other week, it would be a good idea to schedule even more one on one time with your child. This quality time together will ensure that your relationship flourishes, which will help your child thrive, too.

Chapter Ten:

Your Child In Other's Care

Leaving your child in the care of others can be a highly stressful experience, especially if you know that your child tends to struggle with various circumstances due to their behavioral disorder. You may be concerned that others will not understand how to deal with your child's outbursts, how to care for their needs, or that the overall experience will be negative. It can also be worrisome that if your child has one negative experience, they may be less inclined to stay peacefully with others in fear of procuring another negative experience. Regardless, there will be times that you need to leave your child in someone else's care. Whether it be to take them to school or to have a babysitter look after them as you go to work or any other reason that you may need to leave them.

Working with your child and their caregiver enables you to support your child in thriving and upholding a positive experience in the care of others. Additionally, anytime they find themselves in new situations that you are not a part of, they are more likely to grasp the skills required to navigate those situations in a positive manner.

Preparing Your Child for Other's Care

Leaving your child in the care of others starts by preparing your child for that experience. As with anything, you want to do so by discussing what is about to happen, and by setting clear expectations. There are two types of expectations you should discuss, the expectations you have of your child, and any expectations that your child may have regarding the approaching situation.

The expectations you have of your child should reflect similarly to the expectations of the person who will be taking care of them. For example, if they are going to school, you should explain that you expect your child to listen to the teacher and that the teacher is going to expect them to sit in their chair, listen, and complete their classwork. Now, your child is aware of what will be expected of them, and they understand what they must do in order to effectively navigate that experience. You can also let them know what will happen if they don't fulfill those expectations, so that they are aware of what consequences they will be facing if they do not comply.

You should also help your child prepare by letting them know what they can expect of the situation. Tell them what types of people they may meet, what they might see, hear, taste, and touch, and otherwise fill them in on what the experience might be like. You can also provide your child with guidance on how they can navigate any troubling experiences they may stumble across, so they are aware of what they need to do in advance and become less prone to any negative responses.

Preparing Other's to Care for Your Child

Just as you have to prepare yourself or your child for shared experiences, it is also important to prepare anyone caring for your child. You should always clearly communicate your child's challenges, triggers, and any other difficulties they face, as well as how they tend to behave when these experiences arise. The clearer you are about how they are likely to behave, the easier it will be for their caregiver to navigate situations with your child.

Offering As Much Support As Possible

As your child adapts to new situations with different caregivers, it is helpful for you to offer the same level of support that you would if they were learning a new skill. Just as your child may learn how to ride a bike, they also need to develop an aptitude to navigate any new situations or new people being in their presence and holding authority over them. The key here is to be involved as much as you need to be initially whilst teaching your child to respect the caregiver and their authority, also. When your child is in the care of the new caregiver, you must fall back as *second* in command. Your child should always know to trust and respect you, but they should also know that their teacher, babysitter, or other caregiver has as much authority as you do when you are not present. This teaches your child to respect authority and thrive in the care of others, which makes adapting to these new situations far easier.

Mentally Preparing for the Separation

If you are going to be leaving your child in someone else's care on an ongoing basis, such as if they have joined a new daycare or a new school, you will want to mentally prepare for the situation as much as possible. For yourself, rehearsing how things need to go in your mind ensures you are ready for what needs to happen and that you are mentally organized for the various challenges you are likely to face. For your child, make discussing the upcoming change a part of your routine, as you mentally prepare your child for said changes. The sooner you start talking about it, and the more you talk about it, the more your child will warm up to the idea of what lies ahead, and the easier it will be for them to adapt to those ideas.

Reuniting With Your Child After Time Away

After you have spent time away from your child, it is important that you always take time to reunite with your child following that time away. The time spent reuniting should be concentrated toward your child familiarizing back into your presence, and accommodating a positive experience with you again. After the shift, your child will mentally switch from receiving guidance from their other caregiver, to receiving guidance from you. It also helps them mentally and emotionally settle into the change of environments, making it easier for them to move into the new activity you will be undertaking together.

A great way to reunite with your child after time away is to have a specific routine you do together when you first see them again. For example, hugging your child, helping them into the car, and talking to them about their day as you drive home. This simple routine can be followed with consistency and can provide your child with the ability to mentally adjust to being back in your care again. Thus, they will be more likely to listen for the rest of the day.

Conclusion

Raising a neurodivergent child can remain challenging, as you are regularly dealing with acts of defiance and many other various challenges. You may find yourself struggling with knowing what to say and how to act when your child starts behaving poorly, which inevitably leads to your child struggling, too. Learning how to effectively navigate disobedience and challenging encounters with your child enables you to teach them how to navigate these engagements, as well. This creates the opportunity for you both to traverse through troubling situations with greater ease, and welcome a more peaceful parenting experience.

The process of raising children is troubling, never mind raising a child who has greater challenges regulating themselves. Regardless of how overwhelming and troubling it may be at times, you love your child unconditionally, and you aspire to do everything in your power to create a positive, meaningful childhood for them. Creating this experience starts with you recognizing your own needs as a parent, before understanding what your child's needs are and how those needs can be fulfilled by you in a reasonable manner. It is also essential to identify ways that you can teach your child to fulfill their own desires, especially those that are unique to them as these will be requirements that they are less likely to learn about in other areas of life.

As you begin to tailor your parenting style to your child and teaching them how to successfully integrate with the world around them, you will find yourself having far more fun raising your child. The once-stressful environment you have become familiarized with will become more peaceful as you all learn to work simultaneously in harmony and create a peaceful, positive experience with each other.

It is extremely important that you start practicing all of the techniques taught in this book with consistency, as consistency is crucial to your ability to teach your child new habits. Your consistency will also help both yourself and your child recognize these techniques as being positive and useful tools, encouraging far more positive responses to them over time. Before you know it, you will both anticipate the positive side effects of your changed approach, empowering your child to push through and navigate any struggles in a positive manner.

Lastly, I encourage you to always keep learning about your child and their needs and to continue implementing peaceful practices as often as possible. In doing so, you will drastically improve your quality of life, and the quality of life of your child, too.

Before you go, I ask that you please take a moment to review 'My Defiant Child' on Amazon. Your honest feedback would be greatly appreciated, as it supports other parents with discovering the knowledge in this book, and it helps me with creating more excellent titles for you.

Thank you, and best of luck with your peaceful parenting endeavor! I sincerely believe that you are fully willing and capable to gift your child the loving upbringing they deserve!

CPSIA information can be obtained
at www.ICGtesting.com
Printed in the USA
BVHW040226020921
615894BV00020B/332